LIGHT & SHADOWS
Optical Illusion in Quilts

Susan McKelvey

C & T Publishing
Lafayette, California

Copyright © 1989 by Susan McKelvey

Photography by Sharon Risedorph
San Francisco, California

Illustration and Design by Helen Young Frost
Tucson, Arizona

Edited by Sayre Van Young
Berkeley, California

Published by C&T Publishing
P.O. Box 1456
Lafayette, California 94549

ISBN: 0-914881-20-5

Library of Congress Catalog Card No: 88-72134

In memory of my mother,
Josephine McLaren Richardson

ACKNOWLEDGMENTS

$\blacklozenge$

I am grateful for the enthusiasm you, the many quilters I have taught, have shown for playing with color. Your willingness to cross new barriers has inspired me to compile these projects so that others may enjoy the thrill of experimenting. The women of my Color Study Group, whose quilts appear in this book, deserve a special thanks:

Linda Baker	Shirley McFadden
Vicki DeVilbiss	Susan Miller
Sue Diachenko	Audrey Quinn
Nancy Hahn	Dot Reise
Jeannette Haynes	Lynn Reise
Nina Lord	

They accepted my invitation and challenge to experiment with optical illusion and became a cohesive group, supporting and inspiring each other. We worked together for over a year, and I am grateful for their dedication and proud of their accomplishments. I am especially indebted to Mary Sharp, who quilted for me, and to the friends who lent their quilts: Judy Smith, Judy Spahn, and Kris Verbrugghe-Vansteenkiste. And last, but never least, I am grateful to Doug, Leslie, and Scott McKelvey, without whose love and patience I could not write.

Contents

◆

GOING BEYOND
TWO-DIMENSIONAL QUILTS

◆

Quilts are two-dimensional. They lie flat on beds or against walls. Sometimes the quilting creates a slight third dimension because it puffs and wrinkles the fabric. Sometimes relief appliqué or trapunto adds a third dimension, but for the most part, quilters have not attempted to add three-dimensional effects to their quilts until recently.

And that is what *Light and Shadows* is all about: using traditional designs and controlling color to create the optical illusion of depth. This book grew out of experiments and workshops I have conducted using my earlier work, *Color for Quilters*. In that book, I suggested quilters try many color experiments. The projects in this book expand upon those experiments and are designed to show you how to achieve optical illusions in quilts.

Light and Shadows is intended for those quilters who want to go on learning. It is not only about modern quilt design. In fact, many of the designs illustrated here are traditional, even old-fashioned, in flavor. It focuses on adding interest to your quilts by adding illusions of depth, movement, or change. This book will help you learn how color can add a fresh excitement to your quilts, whether traditional or contemporary.

COLOR CREATES DEPTH

◆

I t is color which creates the illusion of light and shadow, depth or transparency, in quilts. After you select a design which lends itself to optical illusion, you must know how to choose and place colors to fully achieve that illusion.

In this section, therefore, we will go over some important color principles which you need to understand before beginning to design.[1] The four principles of value, intensity, warmth, and dominance will be discussed individually.

Value

Value is simply how light or dark a color is. The best way to understand the concept of value is to see it. Look at the value scales in Color Figure 1. You'll see two scales, one in gray and one in red. Notice how the scales shade gradually from the purest black and darkest red to the palest gray and pink. The word commonly used for value is shade. For example, we generally say we used many shades of blue in a quilt, rather than many values. Actually, shades are the dark values and tints are the light values. The accurate term and the one I will use throughout the book is value.

We can find many values of any color we choose, and it is important to train ourselves to see how dark a color is if we are going to play with the light and shadow of the third dimension. Next to Color Figure 1 is a blank set of boxes. Try pasting up your own example of a value scale similar to the two given, using your own fabric.

Intensity (Chroma)

Value and chroma are different, and the fact that colors have chroma is what sometimes makes understanding the concept of value difficult. Chroma is the intensity or the purity of a color on a gray scale. Think of the saturated dyes in the fabrics we buy. The twelve colors of the color wheel (Color Figure 8) are the most intense versions of each color, for example, the reddest red or the bluest blue possible. They are the colors with the most chroma, they are the most "saturated" each color can be. They are the **pure** colors. The color wheel is always made up of these pure colors of intense chroma.

These pure colors can be changed in several ways. As in Color Figure 1, we can vary their value by making them lighter or darker. We also can vary their intensity by making them grayer (changing their chroma).

A grayed color is softer and less intense than the pure version of that color; blues, lavenders, and pinks provide particularly good examples. The scales in Color Figure 2 show how a pure color looks as gray is added.

When we are choosing fabrics, we thus can use a dark, intense red of strong chroma or a dark, dull red; similarly, a pink can be a bright, clear pink or a grayed pink. The value of the two reds or the two pinks is the same, but the chroma is different. Do not let the dullness or brightness of a fabric fool you when considering value. Think only of how dark or light it is. It is the concept of value that is essential to our discussion of depth in quilts.

Warmth

The warmth or coolness of colors is an especially important color concept because it will help us achieve optical illusions. At the top of the color wheel (Color Figure 8) is yellow and at the bottom is purple. The colors on the right are **warm** colors, the reds and oranges of fire, the sun, and heat. The colors on the left are the **cool** colors, the blues and greens of the sky and the sea. These colors always remain warm or cool in character. However, within each set of fabrics you select, different fabrics will become the warmest and the coolest. For example, look at Color Plates 2, 3 and 4, the three *Cat in the Window* quilts. The pattern is the same in all three, but in each quilt, the warmest color is different. In *Rainy Day*, it is the yellow; in *Stormy Night*, it is the rust; in *Starry Night*, it is the red of the border check. In the same way, each quilt you make, because you are using different fabrics, will have a different warmest color. This concept is important because of dominance.

Dominance

We have discussed three color concepts: value, intensity, and temperature (the warmth or coolness of colors). When you apply these concepts to designing a quilt, you will find that different fabrics dominate your design. A dominant color is one that takes over or becomes the main focus in a quilt. The following guidelines will help you in understanding what will dominate and how to control that dominance in your design. After reading them over, test them by looking at the quilts in this book. Concentrate on which part of each quilt catches your eye first. Then ask, "Why? Is it the darkest? The warmest? The color with the most chroma?"

Color dominance is always changing because many factors go into how colors mix and what colors dominate. These guidelines on color dominance are just that, guidelines. New color combinations bring new dominance. Look at every quilt with color questions in mind and keep asking "Why?" It is the best way to learn.

What Dominates

Value Light and dark colors together, without graduated values between, gives strong contrast. Which color dominates (the light or dark) depends on proportion.

Accent A color becomes an accent when it is used in a tiny amount. A little of a light color on a mostly dark quilt will stand out. Similarly, a little of a dark color on a mostly light quilt will stand out. This can make a color the accent, whether it is a planned or unplanned one.

Dark colors Dark colors tend to dominate a design. Try using them where you want the main design to be.

Intensity (Purity/Chroma) Vibrant colors are stronger than their grayed counterparts, even if they are of the same value. This can also override the dominance of warm colors. For example, a pure blue is stronger than a grayed rose pink.

Temperature Warm colors tend to come forward or advance when mixed with other colors. Cool colors tend to recede. Put another way, warm colors tend to become the main design while cool colors tend to become background.

A Lot of Something This makes sense. What you use the most of tends to be what the viewer sees. Using a lot of a dull medium blue (which wouldn't ordinarily dominate because it is cool and has little chroma) will still make your quilt a memorably blue quilt. It may have accents of warm, pure, or dark, but it is still essentially a blue quilt.

Coloring Exercises

We learn best by doing, so this book is designed as a workbook. I have included graphs of each type of design discussed. The paper is a matt paper so you can color directly on it or use it to pasteup your own examples of the various color and design principles.

Coloring is a wonderful way to practice. Use markers or colored pencils, but remember that the color effect will never be truly accurate. Fabric pasteup is a more exact, though more time-consuming, way to experiment with color. Use the actual fabrics you plan to use in your quilts, and you will get true and intense color effects.

For each concept in the discussion of perspective and transparency, you can color your own examples. Stop after each explanation and do the coloring exercises to help you learn the concepts.

COLOR CREATES PERSPECTIVE

◆

How do color principles help us create three-dimensional quilts? In the real world, we see in depth; we see perspective; we see shadows. In quilts, we must create the illusion of depth, perspective, and shadows. We can do this by playing with color and value to deceive the viewers into believing they are seeing light and shadows.

To illustrate how this works, let's look at two traditional quilt blocks. Of the thousands of blocks designed over the past centuries, most are flat and two-dimensional; few attempt optical illusion. Two do, however. These popular traditional blocks which do set up a third dimension are Baby's Blocks and Attic Window.

Baby's Blocks

If these blocks were real, light would be shining on them from somewhere, highlighting one side and creating shadows on the other. In a quilt, the designer decides where the light is coming from and thus where it would create shadows on the other side. Any color scheme will work as long as we control the values. Look at Color Figure 3; the lighted side is of a light value, in this case yellow. The shadowed side is of a dark value, in this case black. Each block has two shadowed sides, but since shadows don't fall in two directions in the same way, the shadows need to be varied, so we make the third side a medium value, in this case blue. The block contains three values: light, medium, and dark. If the value placement is never varied throughout the quilt, the illusion given is of light shining onto the entire quilt from the left side.

The light side of each block in Color Figure 3 is also the warmest, purest color of all. Therefore, it is very strong. The medium shadow is cool so it does not fight for dominance. The black is dark and acts as a shadow to the dominant yellow. Black is also a neutral (a noncolor) which rarely fights for dominance but tends to become background.

However, the lightest side does not have to dominate. We can play with value, chroma, and warmth to alter the main design as in Color Figure 4. Here are the same three value placements, but the chroma and warmth are changed. Now the darkest is also the warmest and most intense. It definitely dominates. The lightest side is cool and pale. It is the weakest. The medium side is cool, too. So the red is left to create the main design in this quilt.

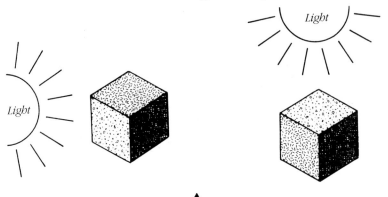

Light And Shadow

Light shining on an object is best represented by light values, and shadows are best represented by dark values. But there are a few other color considerations which may help you successfully create three-dimensional effects. Use this chart as a quick reference when making design decisions.

Light
♦ Use these: values — light
                chromas — high
♦ Use tints (light values) to represent light.
♦ Use "soft transitions….Light naturally has this effect."

Shadow
♦ Use these: values — dark
                chromas — low
In real life, shadows have the qualities listed below. Consider them when choosing colors for your quilts.
♦ Shadows are not just gray or black but have tinges of color, usually a color close to that of the object they reflect.
♦ Shadows have a transparent feeling about them so use soft, grayed colors, not solid black.
♦ The color of a shadow is a shade, not of the color of the object casting it, but of the next lower color on the color wheel. For example, if the object is red, the shadow should be a shade of the adjacent but lower color, magenta. Look for it by moving down on the color wheel.

♦ The edges of shadows are soft. This may be hard to achieve in a pieced quilt where all edges are precise, but you can attempt to achieve it with color, by making the transition from color to color soft and gradual.

Highlights
♦ Use these: values — light
                chromas — high
The actual colors of highlights are even more startling than those of shadows.
♦ Highlights are lighter in value than the objects they reflect.
♦ Highlights are never tints of the object's color but are stronger in chroma. They are almost exaggerations of the color.
♦ The color of a highlight comes from the next higher adjacent color on the color wheel. Look at the red on the wheel; its highlight would be the next higher color, red-orange.

Mist and Distance
♦ Use these: values — medium
                chromas — low
The colors of low chroma give a feeling of distance. These are the grayed colors. The filmy colors are the colors seen in the sky. They are atmospheric, with no substance and no texture. They give a feeling of distance. Don't let fabrics with texture or prints that give a feeling of texture fight with these filmy colors.[2]

Controlling Light Direction: Baby's Blocks

The first coloring exercise is your own example of light shining on Baby's Blocks. Look at Color Figures 3 and 4 as reminders of what you are trying to do. For each:

♦ Use three values.
♦ Vary the direction of the light source.
♦ Vary the combination of value, warmth, and chroma.
♦ Stand back when done to assess the effect.

After coloring a variety of Baby's Blocks, you will see how you can control which part of the block stands out just by changing the placement of colors and values. You are now thinking in terms of light and shadow!

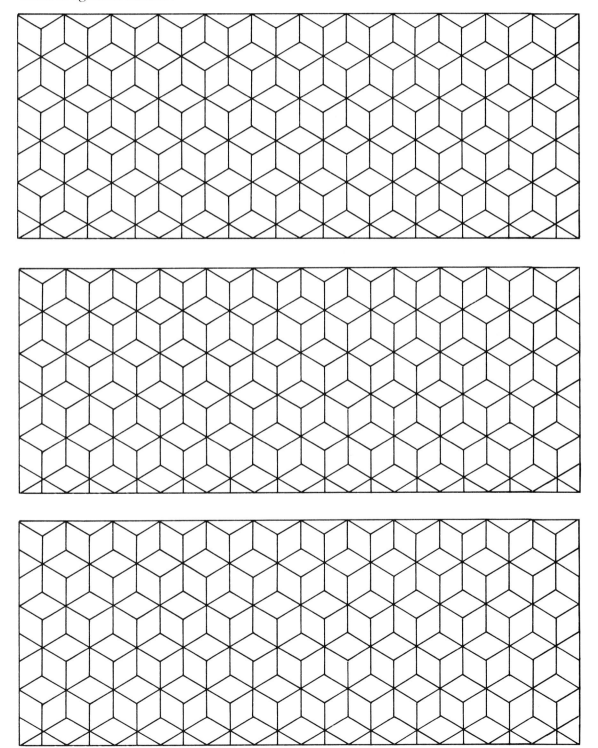

Attic Window

Attic Window is another traditional quilt block which lends itself to three-dimensional design. Look at the three small Attic Window quilts in Color Plates 2, 3, and 4. In each, value controls the illusion of what is seen through the windows.

In *Rainy Day*, the sky is pale and grayed, making it appear distant. Of the two window sills, the lower one is dark while the side is yellow, making it seem as if the light is streaming in from the outside. The diagonal print of the fabric heightens the rainy effect. The window frame and the cat are both dark, but the cat is a warm rust, letting it stand out a little from the window frame.

In *Stormy Night*, the sky is dark and medium, a busy fabric which takes over the picture. Light falls on the lower sill, but the left sill, although dark, is a warm rust; it stands out from the pale grays and gray blues of the frame and lower sill. The cat is black, allowing it to stand out against the paler colors.

In *Starry Night*, the sky is the darkest value. The light bottom sill is prominant because it is the only light space in the picture and thus acts as an accent. The cat, too, is light and accented, while the frame and the night sky are dark. But the red checkerboard border stands out because it contains the only warm color on an all-cool picture.

Controlling Light Direction: Attic Window

Here are Attic Window designs to color. Keep in mind that you can control which part of the design dominates by varying value, chroma, and warmth.

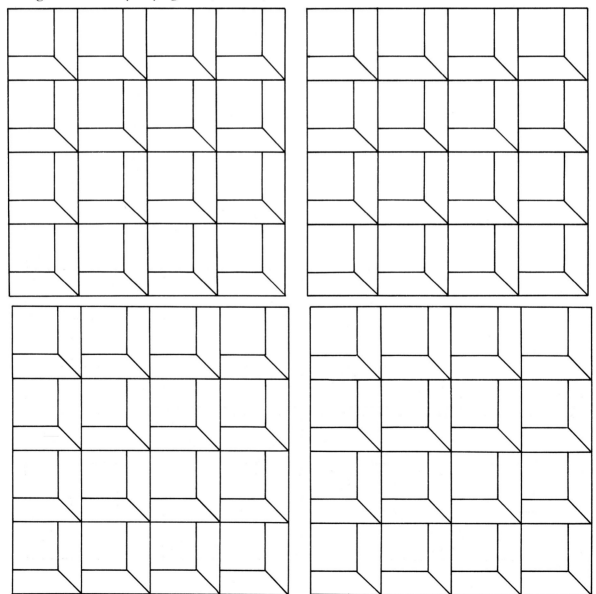

Fred's Spool And Star Blocks Can Be Three-Dimensional

Baby's Blocks and Attic Window are both realistic or pictorial blocks, making them good beginning blocks for work on depth in quilts. It is easy to see how to choose a light source and to play with shadows in these blocks. Many other quilt blocks are not so obviously three-dimensional but do lend themselves to playing with light and shadow if looked at in new ways. With this in mind, try the coloring exercises on these two pages.

Fred's Spool

Color each of the three blocks differently. Do the first as if it is a tunnel leading to a lighted opening. Do the second as if it is a box, and you are looking into it. Do the third as if it is a chopped-off pyramid on which you are looking down. In all three, select a light direction and shade the sides accordingly.

   After you have tried the individual blocks, color the quilt in any way you choose, but decide before you begin what effect of light and shadow you want; then try to achieve it.

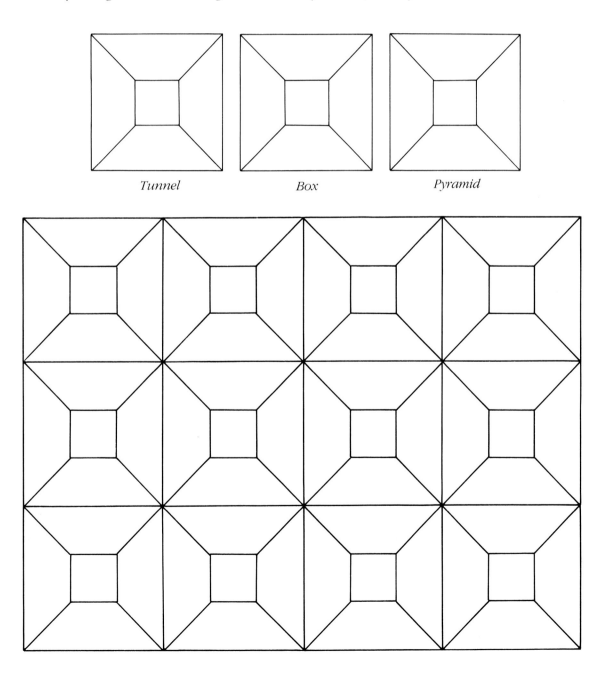

Tunnel   *Box*   *Pyramid*

Stars

Star blocks frequently lend themselves to a three-dimensional look. Color these star blocks as if light is shining on them from a specific direction. Remember, you are playing with value, warmth, and chroma to make some parts dominate and others recede.

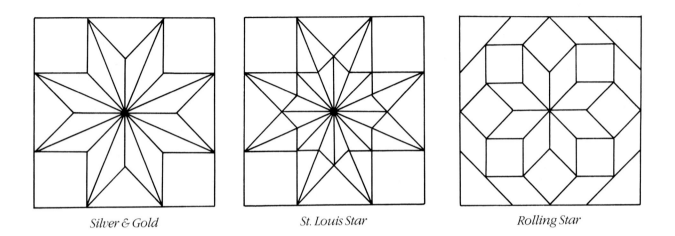

Silver & Gold   *St. Louis Star*   *Rolling Star*

Traditional Blocks Which Can Be Three-Dimensional

These traditional blocks are good candidates for three-dimensional effects when designing.
Trace them, use a copy machine to produce multiple copies, and then cut and rearrange them.
Color each one in different combinations and see what designs you would like to actually piece.
These are just a few of the many quilt blocks which can become three-dimensional once you
begin to look at them in a new way.

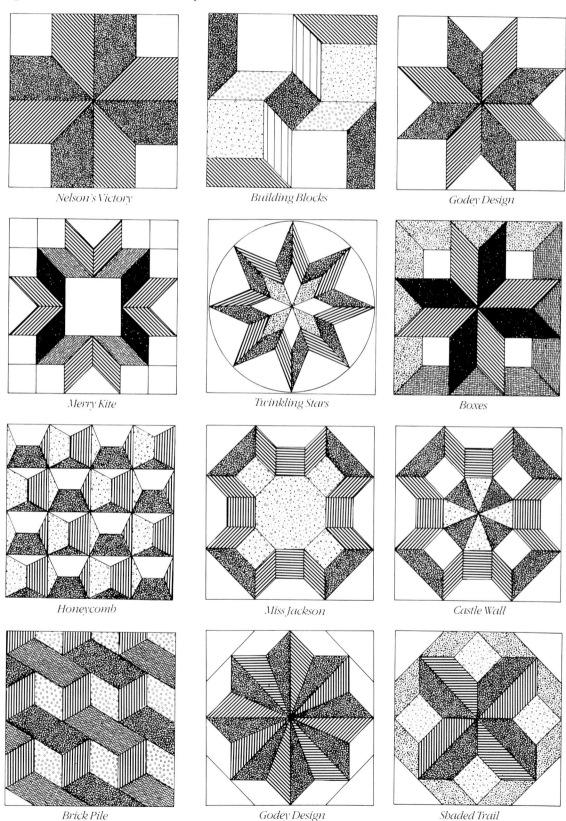

Nelson's Victory

Building Blocks

Godey Design

Merry Kite

Twinkling Stars

Boxes

Honeycomb

Miss Jackson

Castle Wall

Brick Pile

Godey Design

Shaded Trail

Varying Traditional Blocks: Attic Window

On the preceding pages, we looked at traditional blocks that become three-dimensional when we control the color placement. We can vary traditional blocks in countless additional ways.

Consider Attic Window again. In Color Plates 2, 3 and 4, we kept the square block and played with color and value. Here are examples of how you might change the block itself. After you have studied them, use the graph provided to draft new Attic Window variations. Try coloring them in different ways so that sometimes you see **through** them and sometimes **into** them.

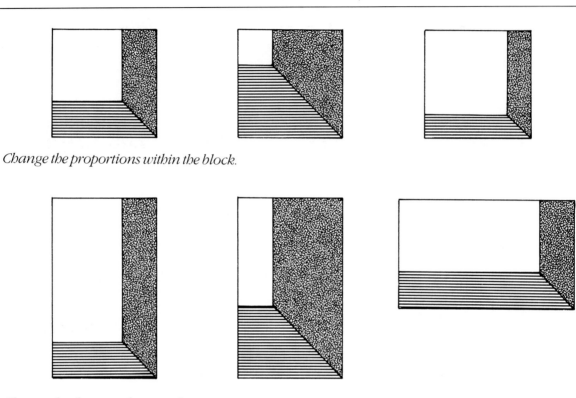

Change the proportions within the block.

Change the shape and proportions.

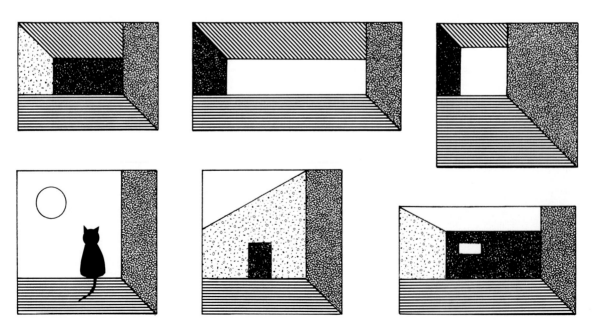

Add an element inside the box.

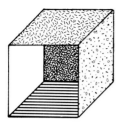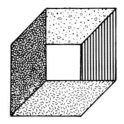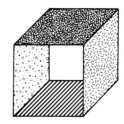

Vary the illusion of the box's direction.

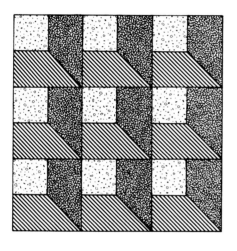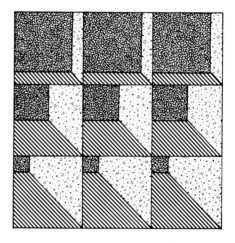

Group the blocks in different ways.

Varying The Attic Window Block

Use this graph of squares to create new window designs; color them to suggest different distance effects.

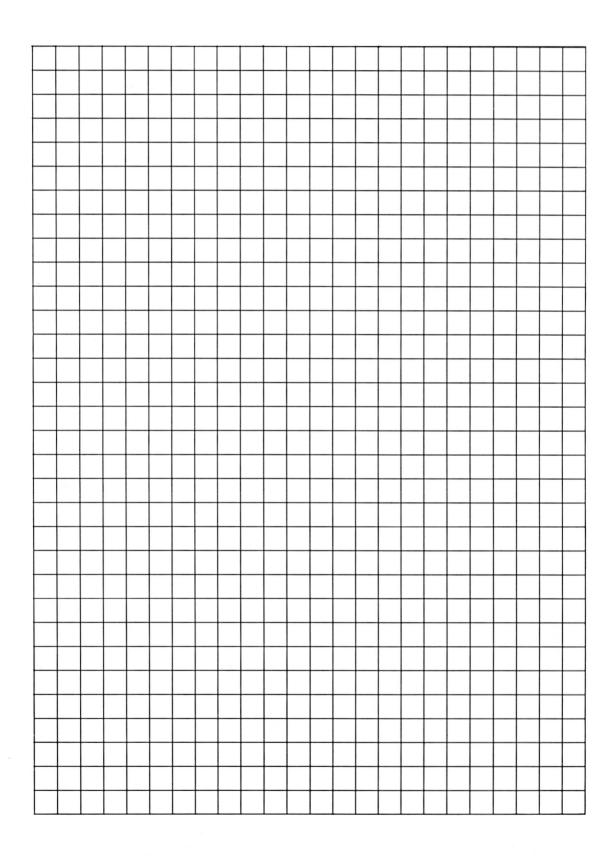

Creating Depth With Triangles

Another popular traditional quilt design is Thousand Pyramids. Successful quilts in this design owe their strength to color and value placement which give sparks of bright colors and light.

The triangle lends itself to many possible variations. *Shadowed Triangles* (Color Plate 8) and *Pyramids* (Color Plate 6) are simply variation on Thousand Pyramids, dividing the alternating triangles into three pieces, which creates a shadow effect.

Study the quilts and drawings 5, 6 and 7. They provide examples of possible ways to play with the triangle to achieve three-dimensional effects. Try these and your own variations on the graphs on the following pages.

Use the graphs to create new three-dimensional designs. Color the small ones, but try fabric pasteup in the larger ones to see what a difference fabric makes.

Creating Depth With Hexagons And Diamonds

More complicated to piece but offering many possibilities for light and shadow are the hexagon and diamond designs. The Baby's Blocks designs you colored in the first experiment with light and shadow used the hexagon in its simplest form. These examples suggest new possibilities for creating more intricate and exciting three-dimensional designs with the hexagon shape.

The diamond, a familiar piecing shape for all quilters, offers exciting possibilities if you consider dividing it to achieve three-dimensional effects. Use these examples as inspiration to create shadows and depth in your quilts.

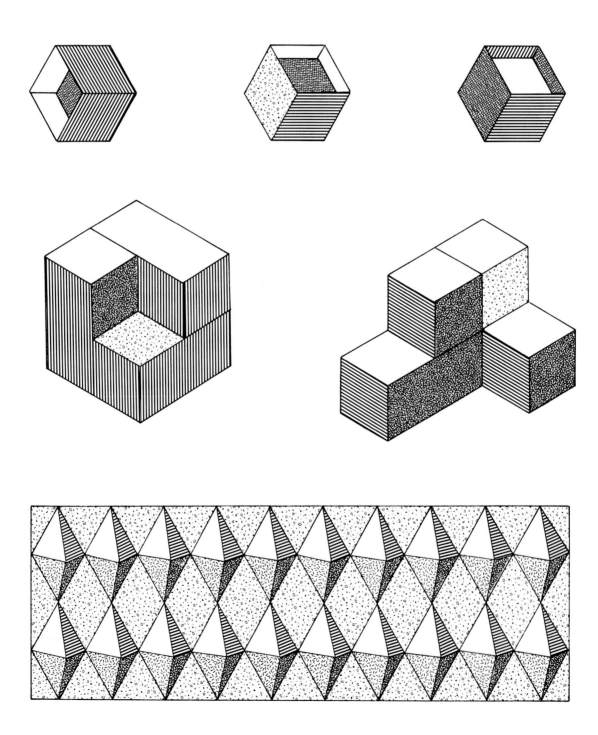

Creating Depth With Hexagons

Use these graphs of hexagons to create new three-dimensional designs.

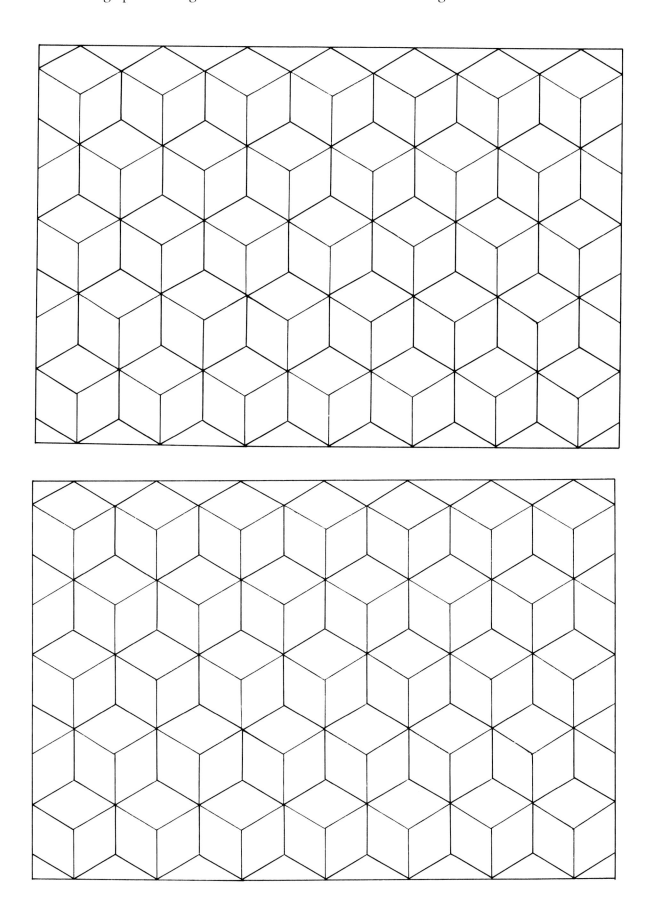

Creating Depth With Diamonds

Below are graphs of diamonds. Use them to try new three-dimensional designs. Color the small ones, but try pasteup in the larger ones to see what a difference fabric makes.

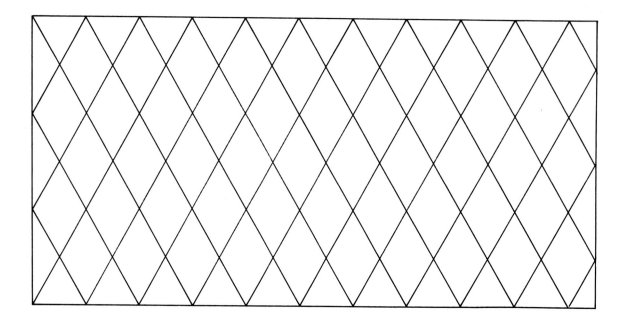

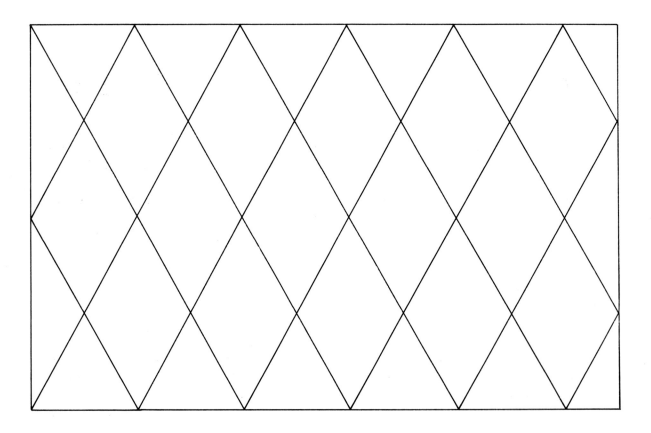

TRANSPARENCY

◆

The first part of this book dealt with color, depth, and shadow as techniques in creating three-dimensional designs. Another optical illusion which holds limitless possibilities for quilters is the concept of transparency. The illusion is that one item is laid over another, and we can "see" through the first to the second. Look at the design in Color Figure 9. It is a row of squares overlapping each other. The squares are obviously not transparent, so we cannot see through them. But just by knowing a little about color, we can create the illusion that they are.

Transparency is an illusion achievable in several ways. In order to discuss these, however, we first need to understand the concept of analogous colors.

Look again at the color wheel (Color Figure 8). The colors right next to each other on the wheel are *analogous* colors. Because these colors are right next to each other, they are closely related and work well together.

Analogous Colors

The first way of achieving a transparent effect is to choose three analogous colors. Look at the row of squares in Color Figure 10. This set of squares matches the one in Color Figure 9, but this time we have added a visible overlap. We have achieved the illusion of transparency by using analogous colors as they appear in order around the color wheel. Under the rows of squares are three analogous colors, blue, turquoise, and green. By using the two outside colors as the overlapping elements, and using the middle color where they overlap, it looks as if one square is on top of the other and is transparent.

Balloon Man (Color Plate 19) illustrates the technique of using analogous colors to achieve a transparent effect. Vicki DeVilbiss makes the six balloons the overlapping design elements. Compare their colors to the color wheel and you will see how using adjacent colors creates the transparent effects:

red/red-orange/orange
red/orange/yellow
green/chartreuse/yellow
blue/green/yellow
blue/lavender/purple

Notice that she sometimes skips over the exact analogous color on the twelve-color wheel, but she is still going around the wheel in choosing her mixture.

The two quilts shown in Color Plates 18 and 20 also use analogous colors to create illusions of transparency. In *Chasing Rainbows*, Audrey Quinn works with the pure colors of the color wheel. Where her strips of primary colors overlap, she uses their analogous colors. In *Mosaic*, Lynn and Dot Reise use blue/turquoise/green/yellow to make the squares look as if they overlap the lattice strips.

Darker Value

A second way to create an illusion of transparency is to choose any two colors for your overlapping design. But where they overlap, use a darker version of one of the colors. See the squares in Color Figure 12. With this method, you are no longer limited to analogous colors. You are free to use a variety of colors. Take care, though; it can be hard to find just the right fabric to achieve the transparent effect.

Lighter Value Or Lower Intensity

Usually when you try for transparency, you combine colors of the same chroma: pure colors together, pastel colors together, and so on. Use this third method of achieving the illusion of transparency if you want a veiled or misty effect. Select a paler or grayer version of one of the colors or of an analogous color for the middle color. This gives the illusion of a sheer fabric laid over a bright color and suggests a feeling of translucency. Look at *Wheels and Things* in Color Plate 12. In it, pale fabrics are used to create the illusion of transparency.

Examples

In Color Plates 25, 26 and 27 are quilts made using these three techniques. Look closely at the quilts to see which method or combination of methods is used to achieve transparent effects (analogous colors, darker values, or paler or grayed colors).

How To Combine Colors For The Illusion Of Transparency

A few notes about color should apply to your transparency experiments, whether with analogous colors or with very different colors.

♦ The illusion will not work well if you mix fabrics of different chroma, for example, dull fabrics with vibrant ones. Choose all clear, true colors or all soft, grayed colors. The examples in this book show both color combinations, and they both work, but the two methods don't mix well.

♦ Select fabrics of approximately the same value when using analogous colors. Two medium fabrics overlapping do not create a pale color, but instead create a color of the same value or darker. You can try a darker value for the overlap when using analogous colors as well as when using the darker-color method. This sometimes helps the illusion.

♦ You can use three values, creating the illusion of a screen in front of the darker object. The overlap might appear hazy, softened, or veiled.

♦ Since warm colors advance, if you are combining warm and cool, the warm fabric will frequently look as if it is on top.

♦ You must play with the fabrics. Do not expect to have the right combination in your collection. Such a specific design objective may require searching for and purchasing the perfect third fabric.

♦ The illusions do not show until they are pieced. Even by laying the cut pieces out, you still cannot get the full effect, so you may have to be willing to "waste" a few blocks while experimenting.

♦ Remember, optical illusions work best from a distance. Stand back. Squint. Take off your glasses. Look through opera glasses backwards. Use a reducing glass. Or better yet, hang your "illusion" somewhere where you and your family and friends will pass it as you come around a corner so it comes as a surprise.

♦ Transparency is fun. Play with it.

Creating Transparency

Try your hand at transparency by coloring the following designs. Felt-tipped markers are wonderful for this exercise because their colors are so startlingly brilliant. They give a stained-glass richness to your drawings.

Each pair of blocks contains one block in which the top shape blocks out the one beneath it and one block in which you can see through the top shape. Color these accordingly, using analogous colors. When done, remember to stand back to see what really works.

Try coloring the border designs by going around the color wheel, using analogous colors.

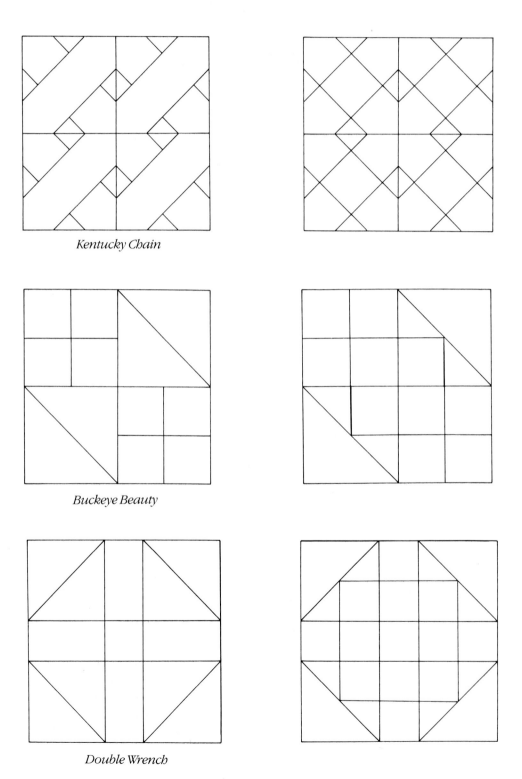

Kentucky Chain

Buckeye Beauty

Double Wrench

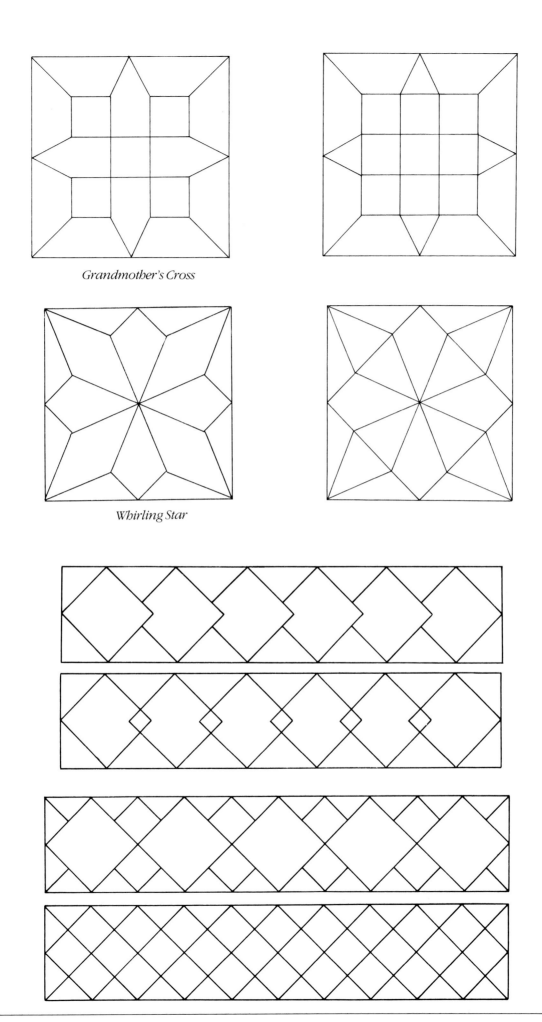

Grandmother's Cross

Whirling Star

Blocks Which Lend Themselves To Illusions Of Transparency

Numerous traditional quilt blocks will work for transparent effects. Once you begin to analyze blocks for overlapping elements, you begin to see how many possibilities there really are. I have included just a few here. Each also represents a category of block types that allows many design variations. Look at these and at the quilts shown throughout this book for ideas.

Frequently, designing on graph paper is a boon to creating transparent effects because the grid shows through the design and suggests new possibilities. This happened to Nancy Hahn when she designed *Shades of Lancaster County* (Color Plate 26). She drew the traditional five-patch Double Wrench, but the grid of the graph paper indicated a possible overlap by adding another patch. She thus hit upon the design you just colored and gave a popular traditional block new dimensions.

Try using graph paper for your drawings, and practice looking at familiar quilt blocks with new eyes. A few samples are shown, with overlapping elements shaded.

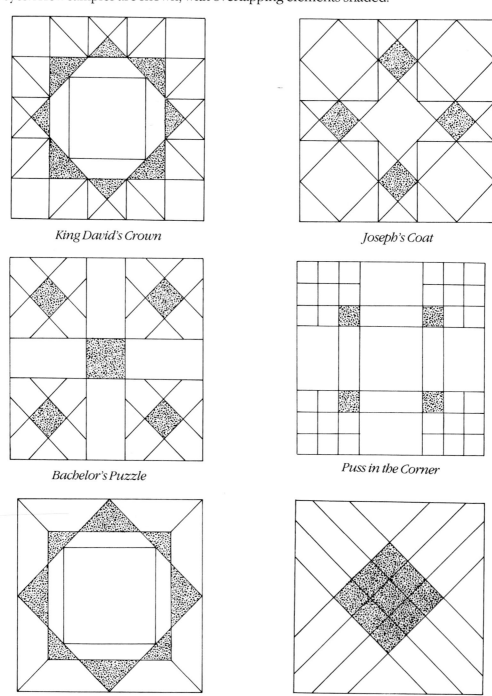

King David's Crown

Joseph's Coat

Bachelor's Puzzle

Puss in the Corner

Mexican Star

Go Beyond The Block

As you saw on the preceding page, one way to find designs which lend themselves to the illusion of transparency is to find designs with overlapping elements. You have just illustrated some blocks which contain such overlaps. But the design possibilities are limitless if you start overlapping even larger elements. Usually the Nine Patch is set like this:

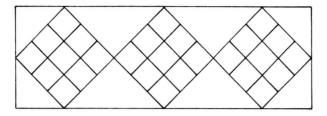

Just by overlapping one square, you can create a new element to play with.

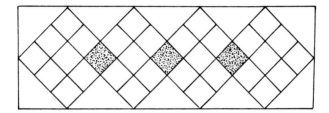

Still staying with simple squares, you can overlap still more patches. The design below is based on a 36 patch, with six squares overlapping.

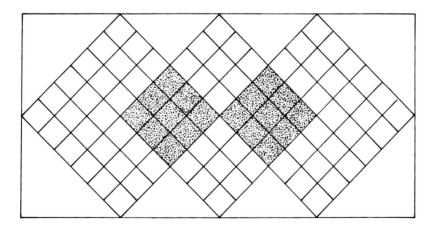

Here is a Double Nine Patch with one nine patch overlapping. These overlapping areas provide wonderful areas to play with gradation of colors or values, possible from dark to light or from warm to cool. The idea of overlapping blocks should lead to many possibilities for transparency.

Try a design similar to one above. Use any scale graph paper. Once you begin to see entire blocks as possibly overlapping, you may go anywhere.

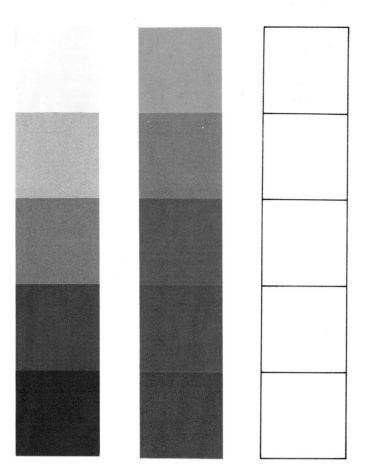

Color Figure 2 Chroma

Color Figure 1 Value

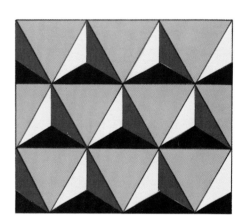

Color Figure 5
Alternate the
pieced and
plain blocks,
using a cool
color in the
plain blocks.

Color Figure 3

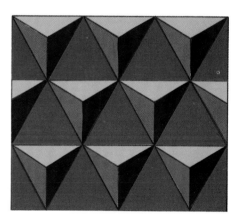

Color Figure 6
Alternate the
pieced and
plain blocks,
using a warm
color in the
plain blocks.

Color Figure 4

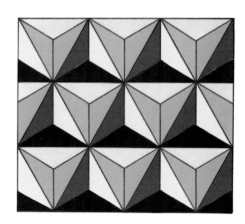

Color Figure 7
Piece every
block, but
alternate color
combinations.

1 Windowsill of Trinkets
40″ x 52″
Susan McKelvey
Millersville, Maryland

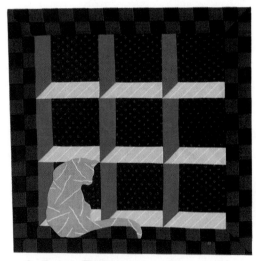

2 Rainy Day
3 Stormy Night
4 Starry Night
24″ x 24″ each
Susan McKelvey
Millersville, Maryland

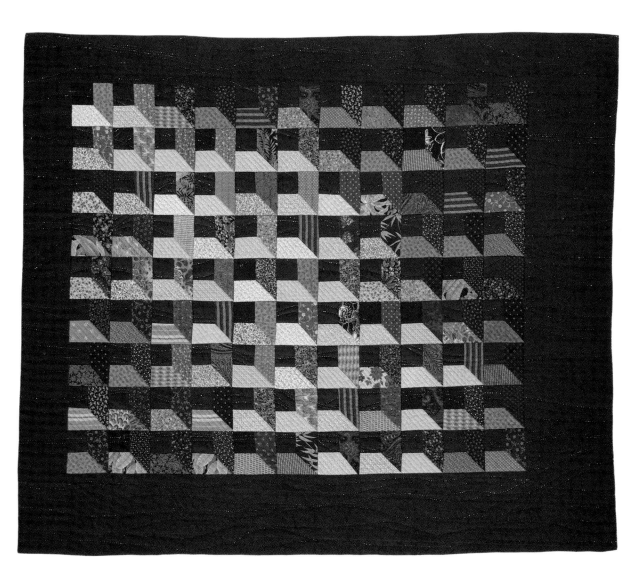

5 Windows on the Cosmos
40" x 57"
Judy Smith
Euclid, Ohio

7 Pyramid Reflections
18″ x 30″
Linda Baker
Annapolis, Maryland
from the collection of Rob Werge

6 Pyramids
36″ x 36″
Susan Miller
Centreville, Maryland
Shirley McFadden
Annapolis, Maryland

28 Shadowed Triangles
40″ x 48″
Susan McKelvey
Millersville, Maryland

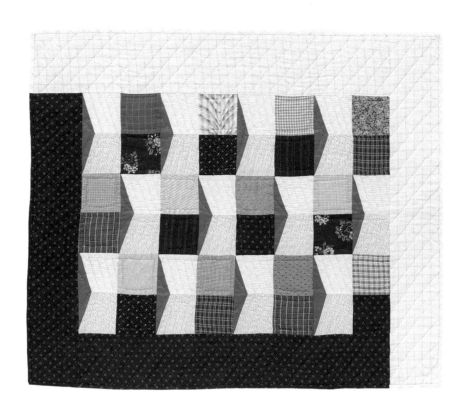

9 , 10 Shadowed Squares I and II
29″ x 34″ each
Susan McKelvey
Millersville, Maryland

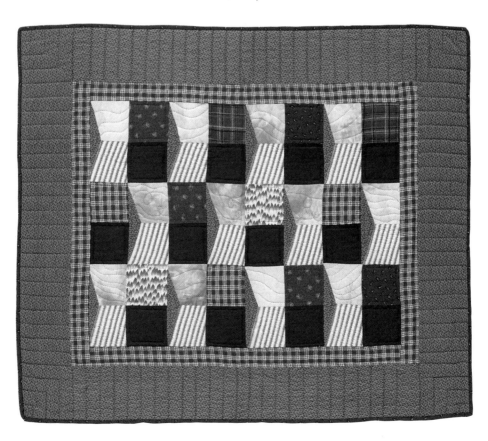

11 Invitation to Oz
32" x 32"
Susan McKelvey
Millersville, Maryland

12 Wheels and Things
24" x 36"
Judy Spahn
Fairfax, Virginia

13 Open Ended
26″ x 36″
Susan McKelvey
Millersville, Maryland

14 Oasis
40″ x 40″
Kris Verbrugghe-Vansteenkiste
Flarelbeke, Belgium

15, 16 Over, Under, and Out I and II
36" x 36" each
Linda Baker
Annapolis, Maryland

17 Floating Boxes
56" x 57"
Sue Daichenko
Bowie, Maryland

18 Chasing Rainbows
18″ x 18″
Audrey Quinn
Annapolis, Maryland

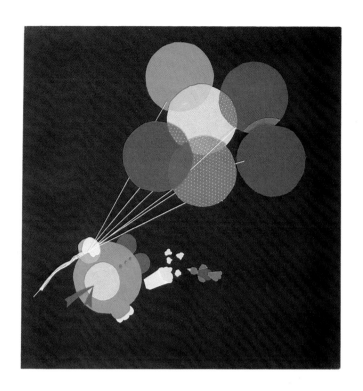

19 Balloon Man
11″ x 14″
Vicki DeVilbiss
Annapolis, Maryland

20 Mosaic
24″ x 36″
Lynn Reise and Dot Reise
Severna Park, Maryland

21 Serene Citadel
35″ x 46″
Susan McKelvey
Millersville, Maryland

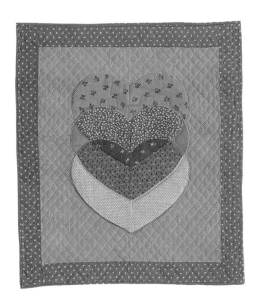

22 Hearts
18″ x 24″
Audrey Quinn
Annapolis, Maryland

23 Old Block Out
24″ x 30″
Jeannette Haynes
Annapolis, Maryland

24 Color Study I
40″ x 40″
Kris Verbrugghe-Vansteenkiste
Flarelbeke, Belgium

25 Diamond Transparency
48″ x 56″
Nina Lord
Annapolis, Maryland

27 Transparency
17" x 17"
Susan McKelvey
Millersville, Maryland

26 Shades of Lancaster County
24" x 36"
Nancy Hahn
Bowie, Maryland

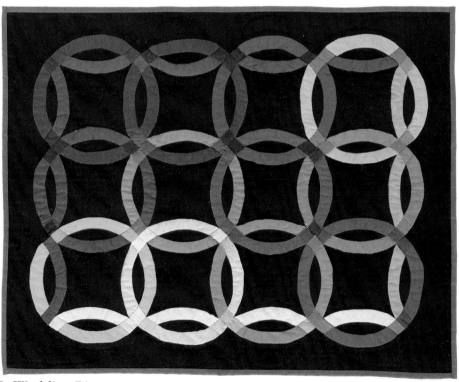

28 Wedding Rings
20" x 26"
Susan McKelvey
Millersville, Maryland

29 Stained Glass Sky
23″ x 33″
Susan McKelvey
Millersville, Maryland

30, 31 Landscape I and II
19″ x 30″ each
Susan McKelvey
Millersville, Maryland

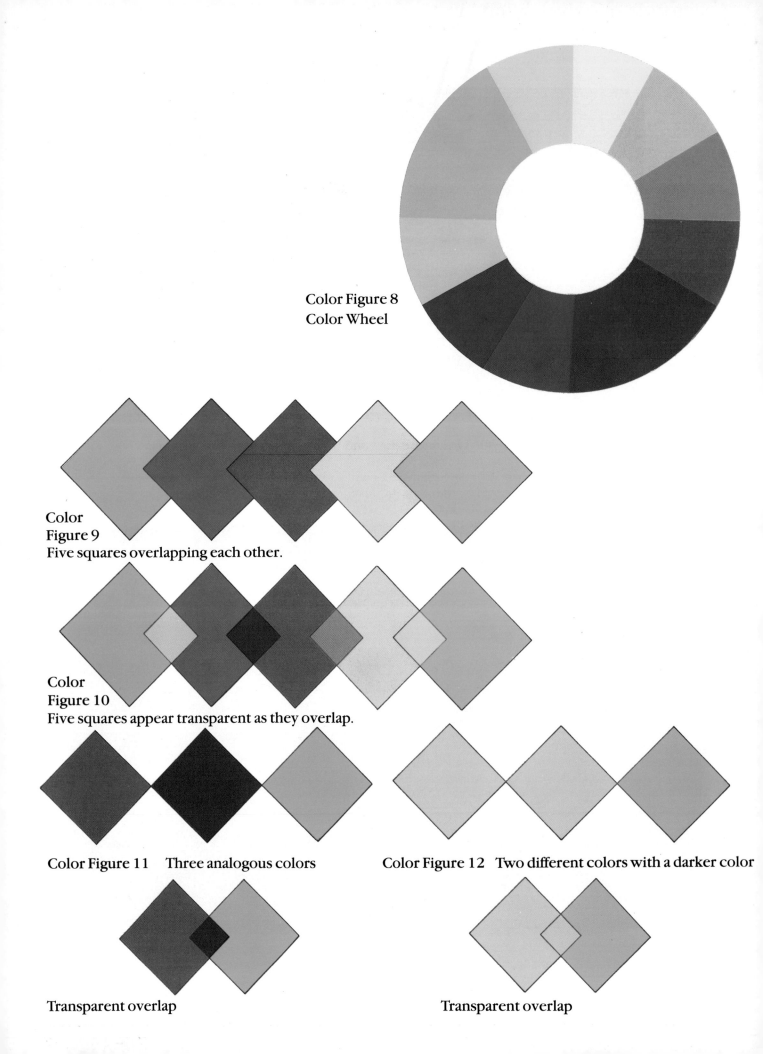

Color Figure 8
Color Wheel

Color
Figure 9
Five squares overlapping each other.

Color
Figure 10
Five squares appear transparent as they overlap.

Color Figure 11   Three analogous colors

Color Figure 12   Two different colors with a darker color

Transparent overlap

Transparent overlap

PROJECTS

◆

In the following section are directions for many of the quilts shown in *Light and Shadows*. For those of you who just want to dip into the waters of depth and color experimentation, these directions should give you a safe starting point.

The twelve projects are divided into two sections: Perspective Projects and Transparency Projects. In each section, both easy and challenging opportunities are included.

For some quilts, I have provided complete directions. For others, I have given general directions and patterns for individual blocks but not detailed instructions on how to make the quilt. Use your own color combinations and block layout to create a quilt uniquely yours.

I have not given specific directions for fabric or color in all projects because I want you to use your own colors and your own variations. This is the best way to learn what colors do when mixed with each other. Use the patterns, but use your own color ideas.

The patterns are given without seam allowance. Add ¼" seam allowance when you make templates. Grain lines are suggested but are not essential since fabric patterns will affect how to cut.

Use this book as a resource and a workbook. Use the characteristics of color and the possibilities of both traditional and original blocks to create the illusion of a third dimension in your quilts. Draw inspiration from the quilts in the color section and adapt the patterns to experiments of your own. And remember as you experiment, adding the third dimension to quilts is possible because color has such limitless variations.

PERSPECTIVE PROJECT 1

Shadowed Squares I and II

by Susan McKelvey
Color Plates 9 and 10

This is one of the simplest three-dimensional piecing projects ever designed. All piecing is straight except one triangle, and that triangle is obtuse and easy to piece. Yet the depth effect is dynamite. The pattern works in any colors and makes a great scrap quilt. It also may be adapted to any size.

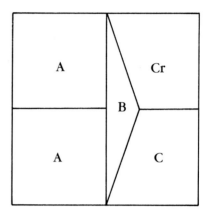

Choosing Fabrics

You are really playing with shadows in this block. In order to achieve the illusion of light and shadow, you must consider value, warmth, and chroma.

Piece A (Top) Here you need a strong color because you want it to dominate. Look at *Shadowed Squares II* (Color Plate 10). I used all reds. They dominate because they are warm and strong in chroma. You may vary each block as in a scrap quilt, but always use your strongest colors here.

Piece A (Bottom) Here you want deep shadow. Choose the darkest value and a nondominant color. I used navy blue. Making it the only solid in an all-print quilt makes it appear darker, too.

Piece B Select a medium value in any color. Since you don't want it to dominate Top A, choose a neutral, cool, or grayed color. It should fall between B and the C's in value.

Piece C Try to find a medium to light value stripe. Notice in *Shadowed Squares I* (Color Plate 9), which I did first, I chose a light stripe which I hoped would give direction and imply light shining in. But the stripe is so subtle it barely works, whereas in *Shadowed Squares II* the stripe is stronger and increases the illusion of angle. If you can't find a stripe, don't worry. Originally I designed the quilt so C and Cr were of the same fabric, not aiming for the diagonal plane but wanting all sky. I got the angle by accident and like it, so either is good. You can emphasize the angle with the quilting lines.

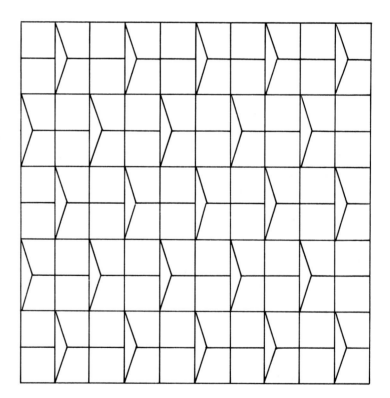

Piece Cr Cr means C reversed. Use the same template for both pieces. Cr is your lightest fabric. It should be airy and skylike. I used a delicate white print in *Shadowed Squares I* and a tie-dyed blue in *Shadowed Squares II*.

Fabric Quantities

The two quilts shown are made up of twelve blocks each, four across and three down. The templates given are for 6″ blocks. The total quilt before borders are added is thus 18″ x 24″.

PIECE	QUANTITY
top A	¼ yard
bottom A	¼ yard
B	⅛ yard
C	⅛ yard
Cr	⅛ yard
borders	¾ yard

Cutting

For twelve blocks, cut twelve of each piece listed above.

Piecing

1. Sew the two A's together.
2. Sew AA to B, with B on the right side. Be sure the dark A is on the bottom.
3. Sew C to Cr. Do not sew beyond the seam line on the B side.
4. Sew CCr to AAB. Do this in two steps. Pin the top half first; sew. Turn slightly and sew the bottom half.
5. Press. Arrange block layout if blocks are different. Sew blocks together in horizontal rows. Then sew rows together.
6. Borders: The borders are each 4″ wide. *Shadowed Squares I* has a 4″ border all around but changes colors on the two sides to echo the light and shadow play of the blocks. *Shadowed Squares II* has a narrow inner red border and a 4″ blue outer border. Play with your quilt and decide what type of border best suits it. The yardage given is, therefore, approximate.

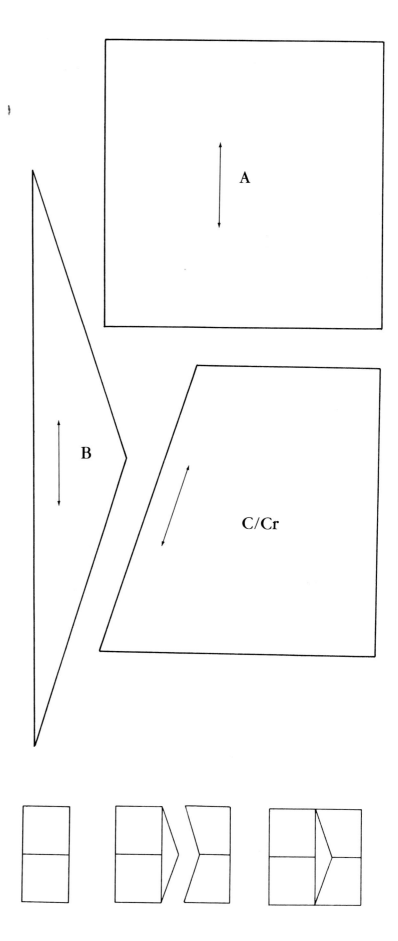

PERSPECTIVE PROJECT 2

Shadowed Triangles

by Susan McKelvey
Color Plate 8

This design makes a wonderful scrap quilt. Use many different colors, just being consistent with value placement, or control the colors as I did in *Shadowed Triangles*. The block consists of an alternating pair of triangles. Return to Color Figures 5, 6 and 7 for the many color and value variations possible. The directions given are for the quilt shown.

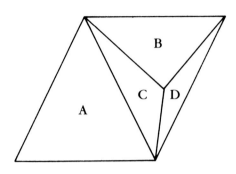

Choosing Fabrics

Triangle A is the piece you want to dominate. For it, use warm, vibrant colors. (I used many different reds for a true scrap look.)

Triangle B is the background. Use pale, cool, or grayed fabrics. (I used light-blue and white prints.)

Triangle C is the shadow of the red triangle. It should be the darkest color. (I used a slate blue.)

Triangle D is shadow, too, but with some light falling on it from the sky (B). It should be of medium value and either cool or warm. (I used a cool color — a medium gray-blue.)

Another Consideration

I also used solids for C and D for several reasons. First I was using such a medley of prints and vivid colors in A and B that I felt the quilt needed some open space — resting places for the eyes. Second, C and D are tiny pieces, and I did not want to have to worry about prints. Third, although I wanted a scrap quilt with every piece different, using prints in all four pieces would have been too overwhelming. Mixing in the quiet, cool solids allowed the vibrant and sometimes busy prints to show themselves off yet not overwhelm the quilt. This quilt may be as large as you want. Just keep adding blocks. Also, the blocks may be scaled up. The patterns given make D very tiny, but A and B are still nice sizes for scraps. D probably could not be much smaller and still be manageable, and scaling up might make A too large. Experiment on graph paper.

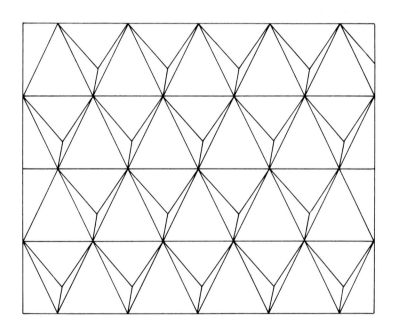

Fabric Quantities

PIECE	QUANTITY
A	red scraps, each 6″
B	pale blue and white scraps, each 6″
C	slate gray — ⅛ yard
D	pale blue — ⅛ yard
border	blue — ¼ yard
	red — ⅛ yard
	plaid — ½ yard

Cutting

Cut one of each piece for each block.

Piecing

1. Sew B to C, stopping at bottom seam point.
2. Sew B to D, stopping at bottom seam point.
3. Sew C to D from point out.
4. Sew BCD to A.
5. Sew horizontal strips of triangles together.
6. Square off the sides in the following way:

   On the left side of the quilt, you need half pieces of red and of the background. Because it is such a small space, you do not need to piece the end background triangle. Using Template A, cut as many of each color as you need. Sew onto horizontal strips.

   On the right side, you need half of background and half reds. For the reds, use Template A. For the background, you want the shadow. Therefore, cut and sew C to B. Attact it to horizontal rows.
7. Sew horizontal strips together. Trim the sides. Do not forget to leave a ¼″ seam allowance.
8. Border: The border width and length will vary depending on the size of your quilt. Miter corners or not, as you prefer.

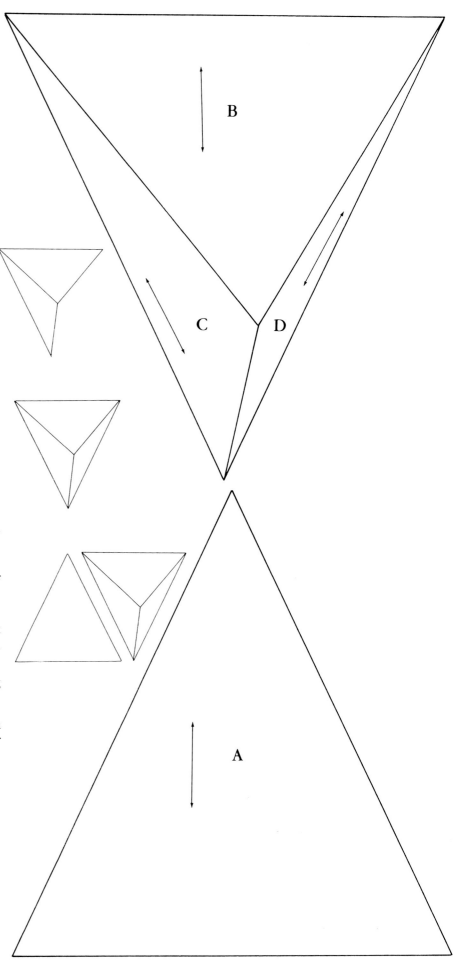

PERSPECTIVE PROJECT 3

Pyramid Reflections

by Linda Baker
Color Plate 7

This small quilt modifies triangles in yet another way to give an even greater illusion of depth. Notice that the pyramid fabrics on the bottom row are the same as on the top row, but they have been overdyed to make them duller than their originals.

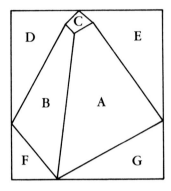

Choosing Fabrics/ Fabric Quantities

Color	Pieces	Quantity
pink for pyramid	A	¼ yard
brown for pyramid and inner border	B	⅓ yard
top of pyramid	C	tiny pieces
pink background	D, E	¼ yard
variety of blues and greens	F, G	¼ yard
brown for outer border		⅓ yard

Cutting

For the bottom row of pyramids (the reflection), use the templates in reverse. Remember to cut half of your blocks on one side of your templates and half on the other.

Piecing

1. Piece A to C.
2. Piece B to AC.
3. Add D to ACB.
4. Add E to ACBD.
5. Add F; then G.
6. Piece the pyramid blocks together in rows.
7. Dye the reflection row of pyramids. Make a large pot of strong tea (six to eight bags in two quarts of water). Dip the fabric in the tea until it reaches the desired color (remember, it dries lighter). Dry. Press.
8. Cut a 2″ strip of outer border brown for the horizontal strip between rows. Sew this on. Add the bottom row.
9. Cut a 2″ strip for the inner border. Sew it on.
10. Add an outer border of 3″ or 4″.

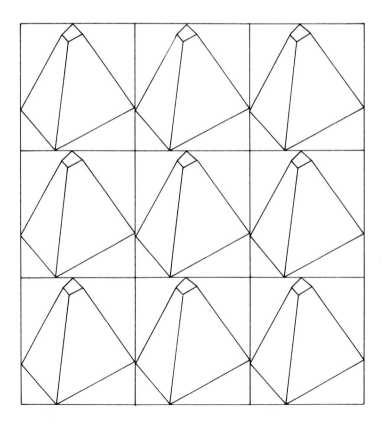

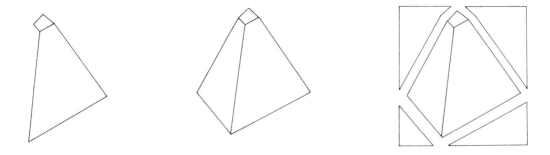

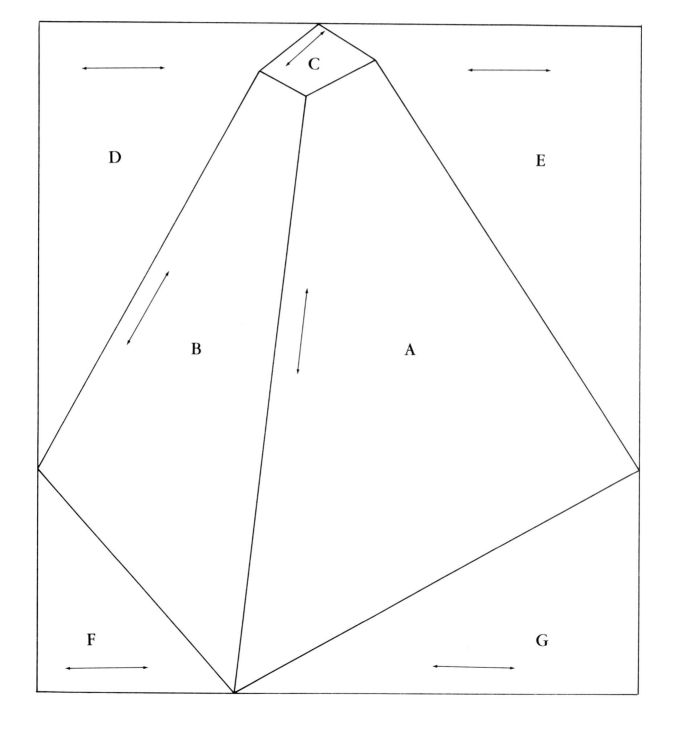

PERSPECTIVE PROJECT 4

Odd Block Out

by Jeannette Haynes
Color Plate 23

This wallhanging has a whimsical twist —
the one block hanging loose at the bottom. Hence its name. It is a variation on
the Attic Window block.

Choosing Fabrics

Use any combination of values and colors
to get open boxes or windowlike boxes.
This makes a good scrap project. You need
several values of each color. Jeannette varied each box so that you see through
some and into others.

Pieces

There are only three templates: A/Ar, B/
Br, and C. Make many boxes; rearrange
them until you get a satisfying color ar-
rangement. Then piece them together.

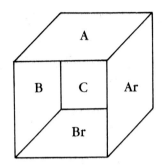

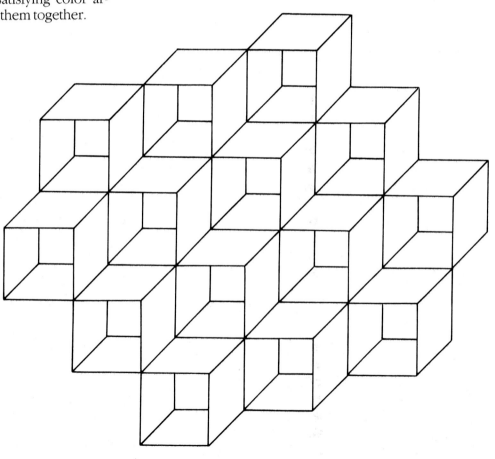

Piecing

1. Piece B and C.
2. Add Br.
3. Add A.
4. Add Ar.

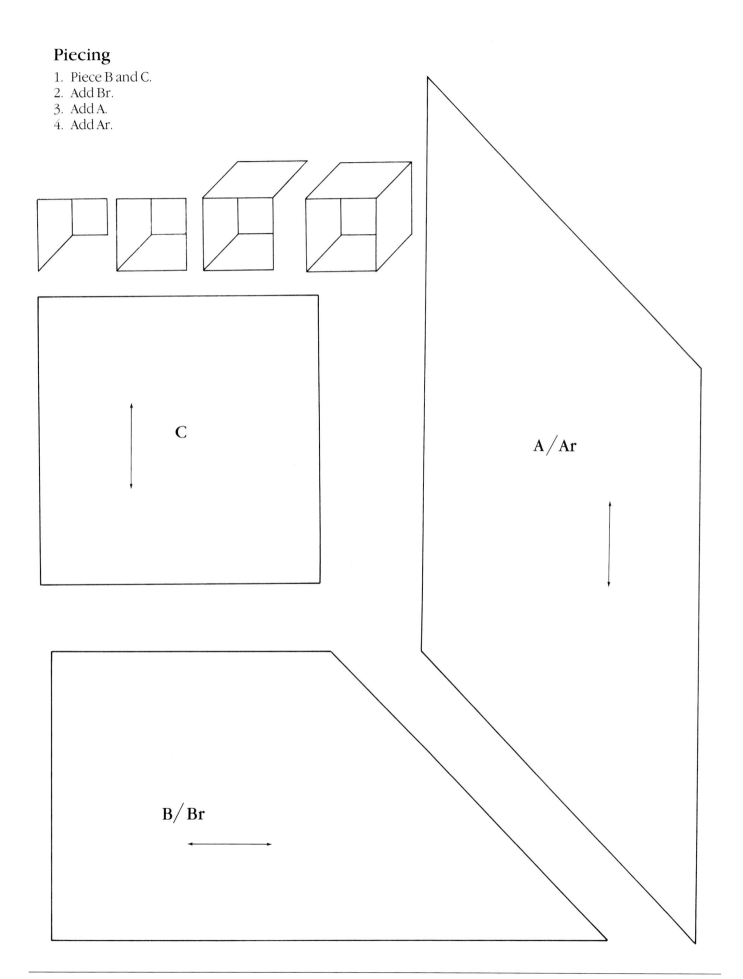

C

A/Ar

B/Br

PERSPECTIVE PROJECT 5

Invitation to Oz

by Susan McKelvey
Color Plate 11

For this project, I have provided the pattern to make one block, but I have not given directions for added borders and panels. The block is versatile and may be used at many angles. Turn it to see the possibilities. In *Invitation to Oz*, it is used on its side with skylike fabric inside the boxes. It could easily be the top to wonderful jack-in-the-boxes or appliquéd treats. Make a few blocks and see what they say to you when you spread them out. Then complete the quilt along that theme.

Choosing Fabrics

Decide whether you want the illusion of seeing into a dark box or through a hole. This determines what value to put in the center (Piece C). The B/Br and D/Dr combinations are two sides of the box. This suggests you choose a light direction and use several values on these pieces to imitate shadows (as you did in the Attic Window block).

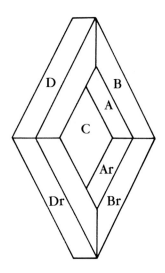

Piecing

1. Piece C to A.
2. Add Ar.
3. Add B and Br bottom.
4. Add B and Br top.
5. Add D and Dr.

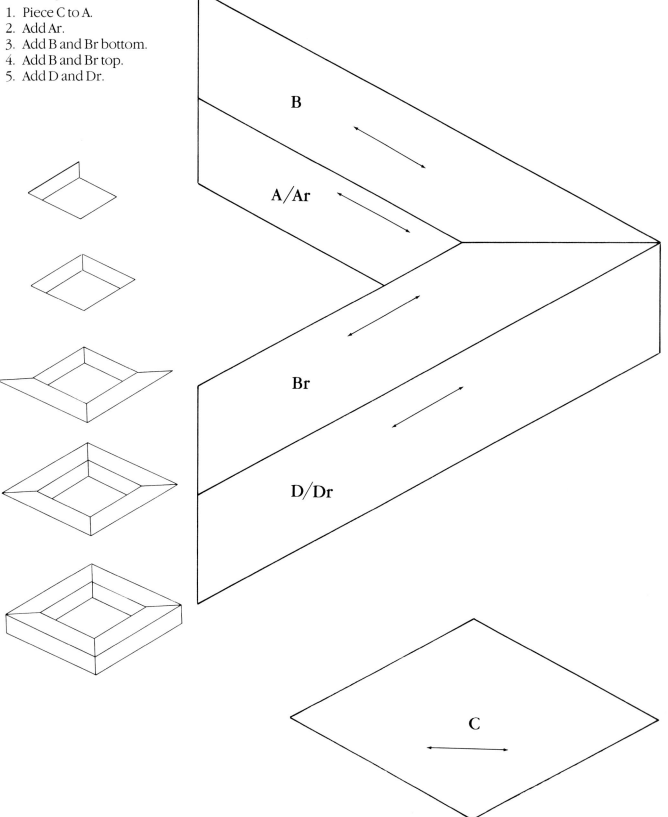

B

A/Ar

Br

D/Dr

C

TRANSPARENCY PROJECT 1

Woven Bars

by Susan McKelvey
Color Plates 15, 16

For a first exercise in achieving transparency by piecing fabric, *Woven Bars* makes an easy, quick project. Cutting, measuring, and sewing are all simple, and you will see your results quickly. The single block can also be expanded into a larger piece with bars weaving over each other. Look at *Over, Under, and Out I and II* (Color Plates 15 and 16). In them, Linda Baker used the same colors on two backgrounds to see how black and white affected the colors. Notice also how she set the simple block on the diagonal, making dynamic wallhangings out of a one-block design.

Choosing Fabrics

1. Select three analogous colors. The two outside colors will be Fabrics A and B. The middle color will be the overlapping color or Fabric C.
2. Work in solids. It helps to begin with pure colors (solids) because with prints it is harder to control the actual color of the fabric.
3. Use black as a background.

Fabric Quantities

For the actual block, you need very little of the colors, about ⅛ yard. Of the black, get enough to do a border or four corners, about one yard. (Black is impossible to match when you run out, so I always get too much.)

Cutting

No pattern is needed. Simply cut squares and rectangles into the dimensions given.

Fabric	Size	Pieces
black	4½" x 4½"	9
color A	3½" x 4½"	6
color B	3½" x 4½"	6
color C	3½" x 3½"	4

Black	A			
B	C			

Piecing

Sew the pieces together in five strips, following the diagram to the right. Then sew the strips together, matching all seams. Stand back. The illusion works best from a distance.

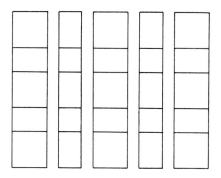

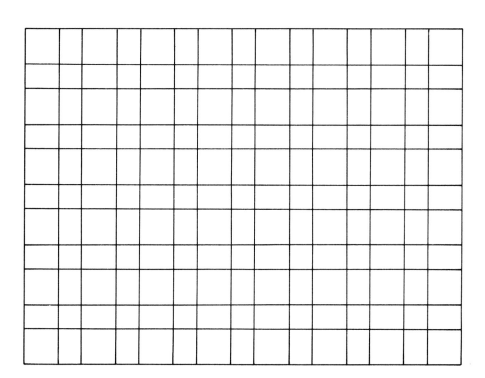

TRANSPARENCY PROJECT 2

Balloon Man

by Vicki DeVilbiss
Color Plate 19

This little appliqué project provides an easy way to practice transparency. Vicki took the simple circle and made it into a delightful child's quilt design. Hers is actually a glued picture 11″ x 14″. The directions below are for making the project into the central panel in a quilt about 22″ x 28″.

Choosing Fabrics/ Fabric Quantities

You need approximately:
    an 18″ square of kelly green for the body
    a 9″ square each of red, royal blue, purple, and yellow
    tiny pieces of each:
        brown (shoes)
        white (popcorn and hands)
        blue (two shades for bird and hat bow)
        gold (balloon overlap)
        chartreuse (balloon overlap)
        red-orange (balloon overlap)
        periwinkle (balloon overlap)
    string or ¹⁄₁₆″ ribbon
    embroidery floss for buttons
    ¾ yard black or other background color
    border — choose any one or combination of the balloon colors

Cutting

Circle A: six balloons and the body of man
        B: arms
        C: hat brim
        D: shoes and hat top

Balloon overlap: Place your circles in an overlapping position. Then trace and cut the shape of the overlap template. Each one will be different from the others.

Appliqué

The patterns are given without seam allowances. For hand appliqué, add ¼″ to fold under. For machine appliqué, stabilize with a fusible stiffener and use satin stitch in matching colors.

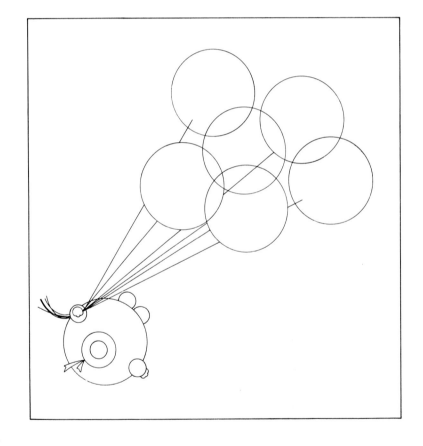

TRANSPARENCY PROJECT 3

Shades of Lancaster County

by Nancy Hahn
Color Plate 26

This quilt has an Amish feeling because Nancy limited herself to the blues, greens, and purples of traditional Amish quilts. She searched out and included many different hues but stayed with vibrant, intense colors. She then tried for as many variations on the transparency theme as she could. The block is a modified *Double Wrench*. Nancy made all of the blocks, then decided on placement by spacing the two strongest blocks in the opposite corners. She also tried to grade from purples through blues to blue-greens across the quilt.

The blocks are 7½".

The lattice of black between them is 1½" wide.

The inner purple border is 2".

The outer black border is 4".

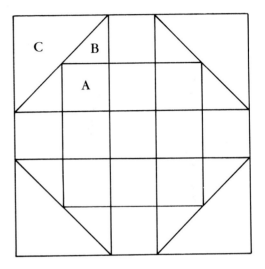

Choosing Fabrics/Fabric Quantities

blocks: ⅛ yard each of twelve sets of three analogous colors

black: 1½ yard

inner border: ½ yard

Cutting

For each block, use three analogous colors and black.

Color	Piece	Quantity
black	C	4
black	A	5
outside color 1	B	8
outside color 2	A	4
overlap color 3	A	4

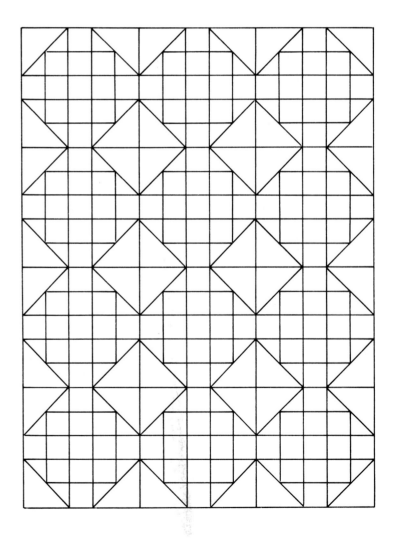

Piecing

This is all straight-sided piecing. Sew triangular units together; then sew rows together.

1. Piece four corner BAB units.
2. Add four C's to BAB units.
3. Piece a five-unit AAAAA strip.
4. Piece two AA strips to go between BABC units.
5. Combine three units: BABC — AA — BABC
6. Sew rows together.

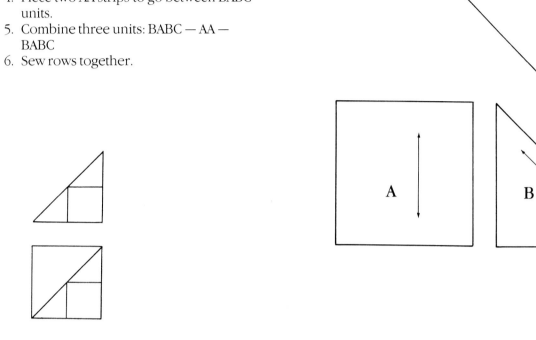

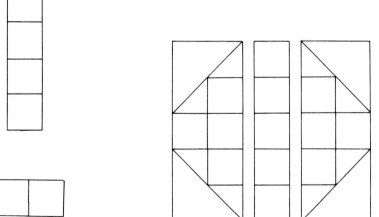

TRANSPARENCY PROJECT 4

Mosaic

by Lynn Reise and Dot Reise
Color Plate 20

This quilt sparkles with color; the illusion of transparency is carried out simply by using four analogous colors: yellow, green, two turquoises, and blue. The pattern is all straight piecing, allowing you time to experiment with color. General directions and patterns are given. Play with the overlap effect on your own.

Choosing Fabrics

Find either four analogous colors or three (including several values of the middle color). Color this project on graph paper before attempting to cut fabric.

Cutting For One Block

Piece	Quantity
A	1
B	2
C	4
C	4
D	4
E	8

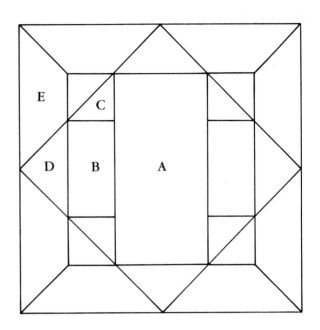

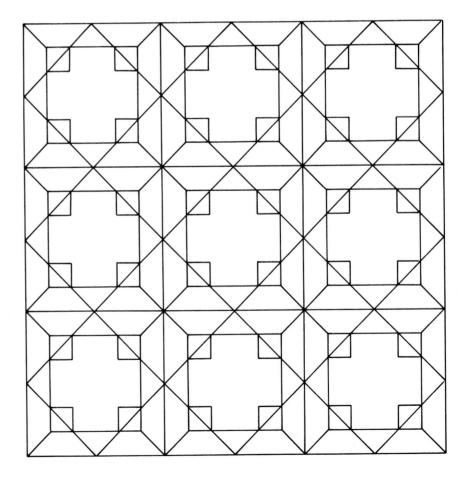

Piecing

1. Piece the two inside corners C to B.
2. Piece CBC to A.
3. Add D.
4. Piece E to C.
5. Add the other E.
6. Sew ECE to the center ABC unit.

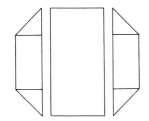

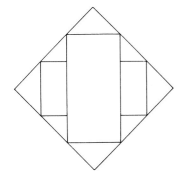

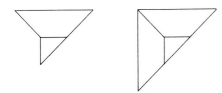

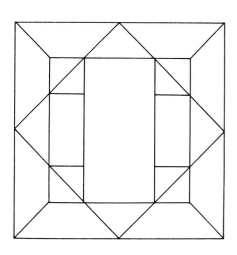

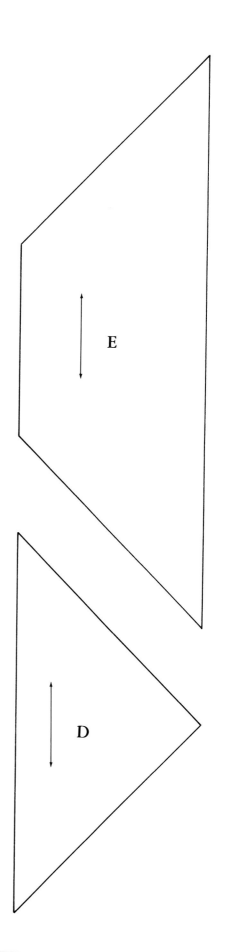

E

D

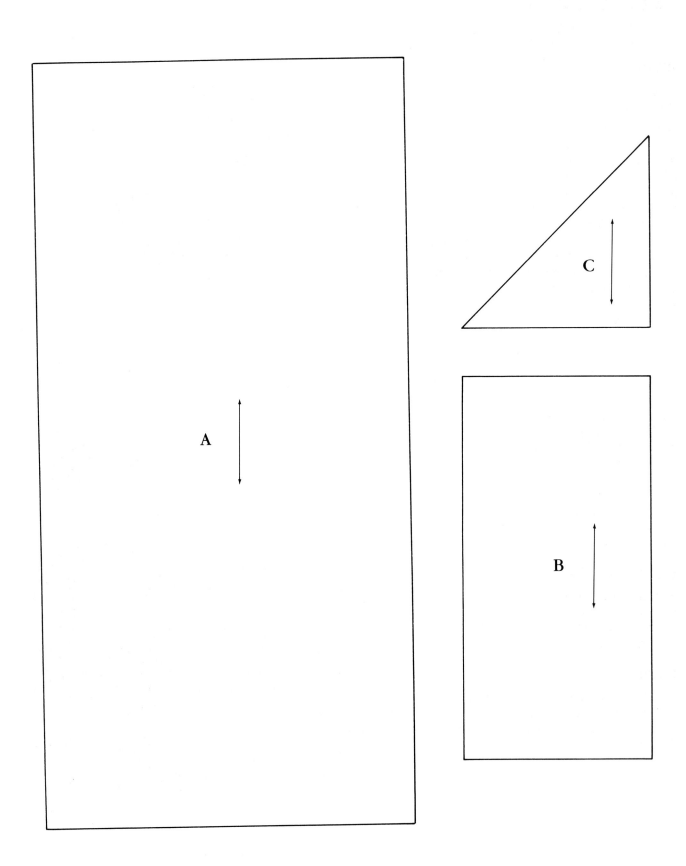

A

B

C

TRANSPARENCY PROJECT 5

Wedding Rings

by Susan McKelvey
Color Plate 28

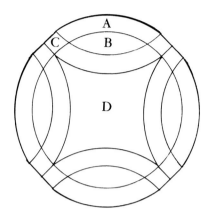

Here's a beautiful way to try transparency. It has lots of movement, and the colors glow as they interweave. The *Double Wedding Ring* is a difficult pattern to execute and is considered by most quilters to be a master-level project. It is entirely curved piecing. Yet it is well worth the effort, and it is certainly worth trying a contemporary approach with solids and transparency. The concept is simple: wherever the circles overlap, you want to create the illusion that one is transparent. Do this in one of the three ways we have discussed.

I did the sample quilt in many colors, but you need a huge scrap bag of solids for this. Therefore, I recommend starting with three colors, two for the circles and one for the overlapping spaces. Or use six colors with alternating rings of color.

The sample quilt is only 20″ x 26″ with twelve intertwined circles, each only 7½″ in size. This is a difficult size to work with, but the results are exciting. The pattern for the 7½″ circle is included here. If you want to work larger, adapt any Double Wedding Ring pattern by eliminating the pieced section of the ring.

Choosing Fabrics

background — one yard
colors — a great variety of many, or if working in only three colors, three analogous colors.

Pieces

1. Make the four templates A, B, C, D.
2. Mark template C with an arrow to distinguish the inside from the outside.
3. Mark the centers of A, B, and D as shown.

Cutting

For this quilt, I recommend laying out all of the pieces and playing with the colors. I use a flannel board or a flannel wall.

Important: Transfer the center markings onto fabric as you mark and cut. This will make pinning the curved seam easy and accurate.

> **background:** cut 12 of D
>   cut 31 of B

rings: cut four of each ring color to form the rings

overlap: cut 62 of C, two for each overlap color. Look at *Wedding Rings* closely. Notice how, even with many different colored rings, each overlaps *one other color* twice. If you are working in a three-color scheme, just cut 62 of the overlap color.

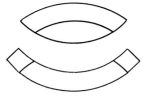

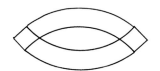

Piecing

1. Sew one side A to B.
2. Sew other A to two C's.
3. Sew AB to CAC.
4. Sew ABC unit to D.
5. Sew another ABC unit. Sew this to D. Do this around the circle.

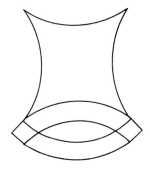

Hints

1. When sewing curves, pin well and frequently.
2. Match center marks on A, B, and D. Pin there and at corner points. Ease (gently) all wrinkles out.
3. When attaching D to ABC units, careful piecing and easing is essential. At the end, be sure the corner point of D is in back; don't let it get caught in front.
4. Attach circles to each other across the top row. Do the second row and attach. Because this is all curves, nothing really makes it easy.
5. When rings are done, you are ready to attach the outside background. Cut strips of background color the length of each side. Appliqué the ring to these borders. Trim excess.
6. I machine pieced and used machine templates. With a lot of pinning and careful easing around curves, it went together quite smoothly.

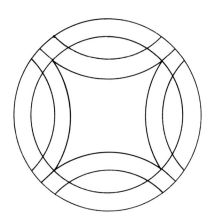

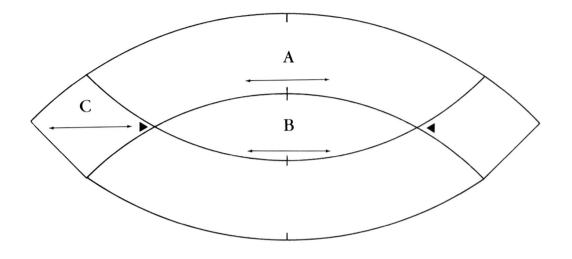

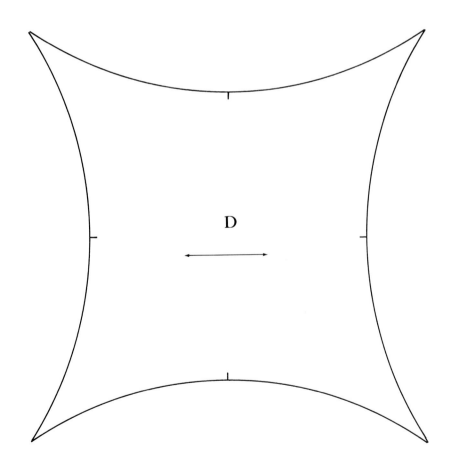

TRANSPARENCY PROJECT 6

Landscape I and II

by Susan McKelvey
Color Plates 30, 31

In both of these small quilts, I played with basic triangular and diamond shapes for different illusions of transparency. The two basic design panels are shown here. The panels are in proportions of 2:12 and divisions in between.

In the two quilts in Color Plates 30 and 31, I used the same panel combinations, simply changing the color arrangements. Then I pretended different elements overlapped and used analogous colors and value changes to give the illusion of overlap. The background may be varied in any way. The simple panels (mine are 4" x 24" per panel and three panels deep) can be combined in numerous ways. Drafting will help you get started. Use graph paper and play with different panel and color combinations. The piecing is straight and easy, but the effect is dramatic.

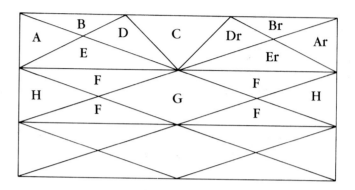

Choosing Fabrics

Work in a limited range of four or five analogous colors. I went around the wheel from yellow-green through purple. Choose several values of each color. Quantities depend upon how many and what size panels you use.

Pieces

On a large sheet of paper, draft panels 1 and 2, each 4" x 24". Draw the lines as shown. Notice that in Panel 1, all templates have reversed templates. Be sure to make them. Panel 2 is much simpler and requires only three templates.

Cutting

This is a design which works best when you cut and try; then retry. Cut several pieces and lay them out to see if the effect is what you want. If not, try again.

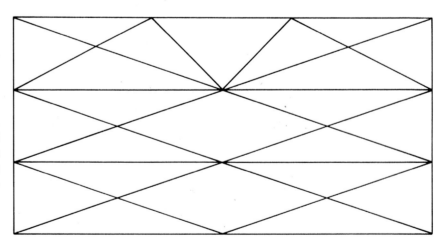

Piecing

The hard part of this is in the designing.
Piecing is easy. You may piece several
ways and still have no pieces to set in.

Panel 1
1. Piece A to B and Ar to Br.
2. Piece E to D and Er to Dr.
3. Piece AB to ED and ArBr to ErDr.
4. Attach two sides (ABED) and its mirror
   to C.

Panel 2
1. Piece H to lower F and its mirror.
2. Piece two upper F's to center G.
3. Attach the two sides (HF) to center FGF.
4. Attach panels to each other in rows,
   matching points.

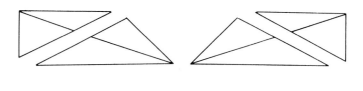

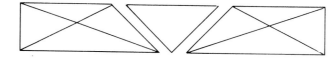

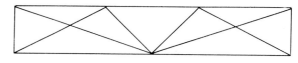

Panel 1

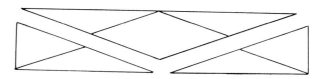

Panel 2

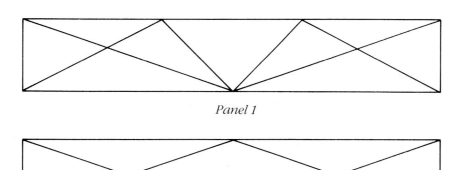

Panel 1

Panel 2

TRANSPARENCY PROJECT 7

Stained Glass Sky

by Susan McKelvey
Color Plate 29

This quilt was inspired by a quilt called *Diversion* by Nancy Martin, shown with patterns in her book *Pieces of the Past*. It is made by combining two blocks: Gentleman's Fancy and a connecting block.

Choosing Fabrics

In order to achieve a transparent look, you need to control colors carefully. Each block is a different color, but within each block, work with several values of one color or of two analogous colors. Refer to the diagram as we discuss color.

Gentleman's Fancy

Choose the values and analogous colors for one block in this way:
- **A** Make this the darkest (a solid).
- **B** Make this the brightest (a solid).
- **C** Make this a medium solid.
- **D** Use a print which echoes the color in C, possibly with less chroma or lighter in value.
- **E** Use a pale print which echoes C but is very light in value and chroma.

Connecting Block

- **F** Use a background fabric. I chose a skylike tie-dyed fabric.
- **G** This fabric makes the gridlike secondary pattern. I used a value darker than the background in the same color. You may want to start something new.

Important

1. The diamond formed by AB should be the strongest element in the block. So, whether you select analogous colors or several values of one color, make the middle brightest and dominant.

2. A or B may be the strongest. However you do it, always make C the weakest.

3. Corner E should blend into F (it basically looks like an overlapping corner). Choose a pale color between C and F to give the transparent effect.

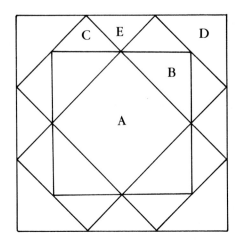

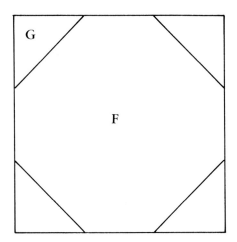

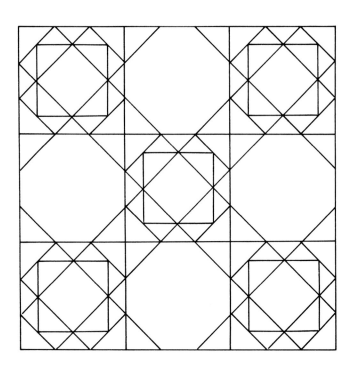

Fabric Quantities

Stained Glass Sky consists of nine differently colored Gentleman's Fancy blocks and four whole connecting blocks, with twelve side blocks of background. Buy one yard of the background color. Of the rest, ⅛ to ¼ yard will be more than enough. Of pieces C and E, you need just tiny pieces.

Piecing

1. Make nine *Gentleman's Fancy* blocks. The piecing is all straight.
2. Sew the connecting blocks.
3. Sew eight side blocks by using one corner G and half of F plus an inch on the fold side (now an open side) to be trimmed later.
4. Sew blocks together in diagonal rows.
5. Add four corners by cutting four triangles from Template H.
6. The borders is a design decision which is up to you.

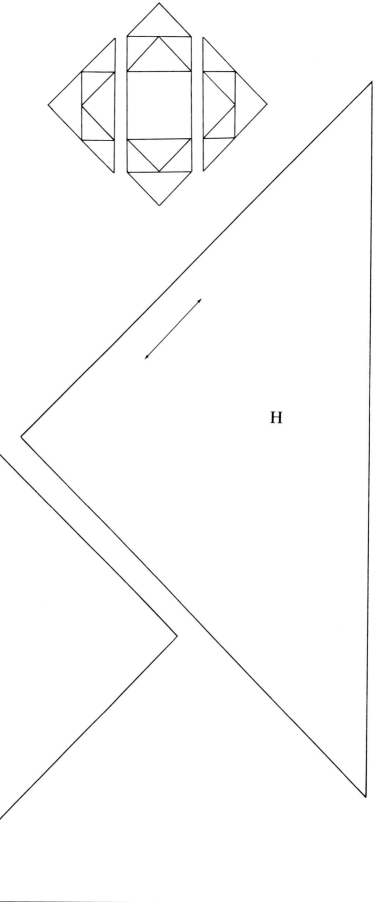

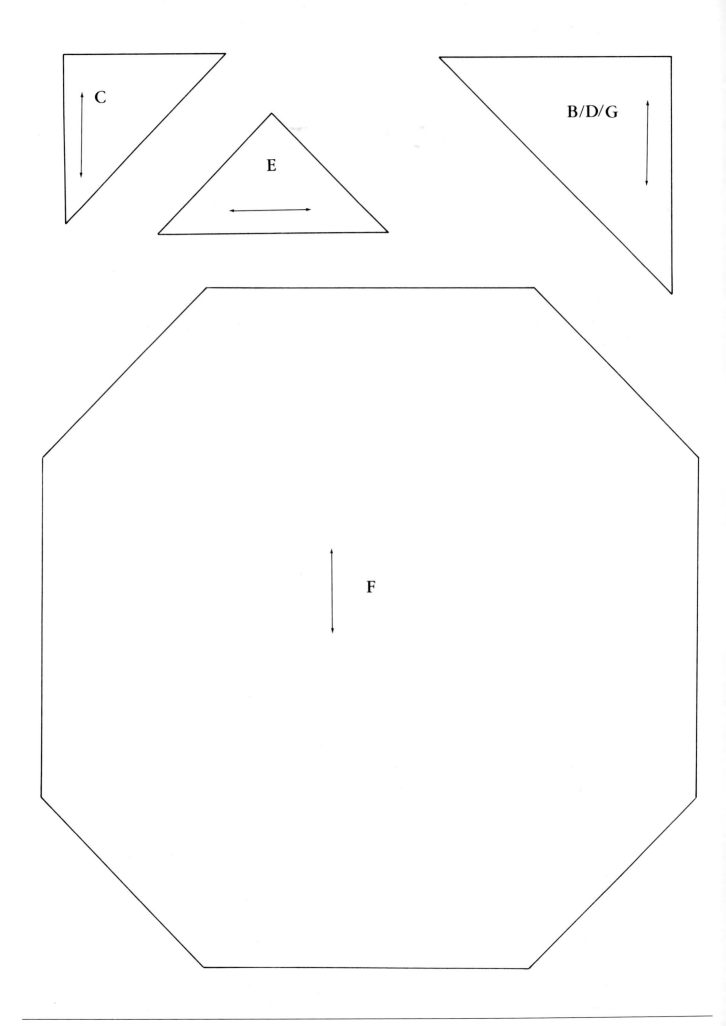

FOOTNOTES

◆

[1]For a complete discussion of color, refer to the author's *Color for Quilters* (Yours Truly–Burdett Publications, 1984).

[2]Faber Birren, *Color Perception in Art* (Schiffer Publishing Ltd., West Chester, Pennsylvania, 1986), page 29.

[3]Jinny Beyer, *The Quilter's Album of Blocks and Borders* (EPM Publications, Inc., McLean, Virginia, 1980). This is a good source for traditional quilt blocks.

The cat silouette is from Amity Publications's pattern "Amish Cats and Rats." Available from Amity Publications, 78688 Sears Road, Cottage Grove, Oregon 97424.

BIBLIOGRAPHY

◆

Albers, Joseph. *The Interaction of Color*. New Haven: Yale University Press, 1975.

Beyer, Jinny. *The Quilter's Album of Blocks and Borders*. McLean, Virginia: EPM Publications, Inc.: 1980.

Birren, Faber. *Color Perception in Art*. West Chester, Pennsylvania: Schiffer Publishing Ltd., 1986.

———. *Creative Color*. West Chester, Pennsylvania: Schiffer Publishing Ltd., 1987.

Ellinger, Richard G. *Color Structure and Design*. New York: Van Nostrand Reinhold, 1980.

Horton, Roberta. *An Amish Adventure*. Lafayette, California: C & T Publishing, 1983.

Itten, Johannes. *The Elements of Color*. Edited by Faber Birren. New York: Van Nostrand Reinhold, 1970.

McKelvey, Susan. *Color for Quilters*. Westminster, California: Yours Truly–Burdett Publications, 1984.

———. *The Color Workbook*. Westminster, California: Yours Truly–Burdett Publications, 1987.

Martin, Nancy. *Pieces of the Past*. Bothell, Washington: That Patchwork Place, 1986.

Munsell, A. H. *A Color Notation*. Baltimore: Munsell Color Company, 1946.

Pasquini, Katie. *Mandala*. Eureka, California: Sudz Publishing, 1983.

———. *3 Dimensional Design*. Lafayette, California: C & T Publishing, 1988.

Wong, Wucius. *Principles of Three-Dimensional Design*. New York: Van Nostrand Reinhold, 1977.

ABOUT THE AUTHOR

◆

Susan McKelvey wrote *Light and Shadows* in response to the enthusiasm of quilt students in workshops across the United States. Their interest in the exercises she presented in *Color for Quilters* encouraged her to gather more beginning exercises on using optical illusion in quilts.

This is Susan's third book on color. Her easy-to-read *Color for Quilters* has been hailed as the definitive quilters' book on color and a must for every quilter's library. *The Color Workbook* follows as a classroom aid and poster for color study, either individually or in classes.

Susan has taught quilting and owned a quilt shop, and is currently the owner of Wallflower Designs, where she designs patterns and silk-screened fabric. She is a member of the New Image Quilters, and her work has been shown in the Baltimore Museum of Art, the D.A.R. Museum in Washington, D.C., and in art galleries in Virginia, Maryland, North Carolina, and Washington, D.C. She travels and teaches quilting throughout the country.

She lives in Annapolis, Maryland, where her life centers around her family and quilts. ("Not necessarily in that order," interjects her husband!) She began quilting in North Carolina in 1977. The first lesson was the *Dresden Plate*. While everyone went home and made one *Dresden Plate*, Susan went home and made twenty! She used all of her scraps in those blocks, had to go out and buy more fabric, and hasn't stopped since. Her interest in color began soon after, and *Light and Shadows* is a direct result. Her hope is that quilters will be inspired to use the ideas in this book to delve further into three-dimensional design in quilts.